I0665036

THE Qe
QUEER EYE
GUIDE

HOW TO LOVE YOURSELF
THE FAB FIVE WAY

PENGUIN WORKSHOP
An Imprint of Penguin Random House LLC, New York

Penguin supports copyright. Copyright fuels creativity, encourages
diverse voices, promotes free speech, and creates a vibrant culture. Thank you
for buying an authorized edition of this book and for complying with copyright laws
by not reproducing, scanning, or distributing any part of it in any form
without permission. You are supporting writers and allowing
Penguin to continue to publish books for every reader.

The publisher does not have any control over and does not assume any
responsibility for author or third-party websites or their content.

Copyright © 2020 Scout Productions. All rights reserved. Published by
Penguin Workshop, an imprint of Penguin Random House LLC, New York.
PENGUIN and PENGUIN WORKSHOP are trademarks of Penguin Books Ltd,
and the W colophon is a registered trademark of Penguin Random House LLC.
Manufactured in China.

Illustrated by Dale Edwin Murray

Visit us online at www.penguinrandomhouse.com.

ISBN 9780593094594   10 9 8 7 6 5 4 3 2 1

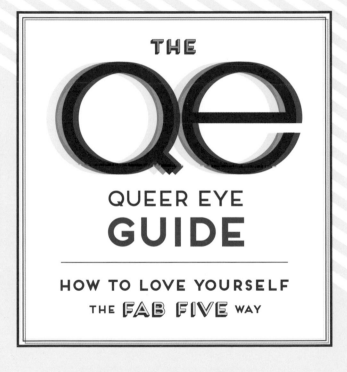

THE

Qe

QUEER EYE
GUIDE

HOW TO LOVE YOURSELF
THE FAB FIVE WAY

PENGUIN WORKSHOP

INTRODUCTION

The ability to see the best version of yourself is sort of like a superpower. We know, it's totally corny. But hear us out.

Self-acceptance is a superpower because it gives you perspective. Most days, self-acceptance can be the hardest mountain to conquer. The road feels too steep, the twists and turns too sudden, the terrain too rocky. But once you reach the summit, you can see things from a whole new vantage point. The way you approach people and the way they approach you strengthens. The way you move within the world changes. Your breath steadies.

That's the spirit of *Queer Eye*, and that's what this book is all about.

Real change doesn't happen overnight. There's beauty in progress, in the journey, and in the smallest moments of life that become uniquely, perfectly, and simply yours.

Never hide from it. Instead run like hell toward it.

Feel-Good Fundamentals

hese days, we hear buzzwords and phrases like "self-care," "self-love," "progress not perfection," and "live your best life" used everywhere—from advertisements to the media to what we hear at school. But what do these words actually mean? And do we use them in a way that is constructive? By redefining these buzzwords to cater to *you*, you'll have feel-good fundamentals to serve as a guide.

There's no time like the present to start. Use the next few pages to take back the power in each of these words:

- **SELF-CARE**

- **SELF-LOVE**

- **PROGRESS NOT PERFECTION**

- **LIVE YOUR BEST LIFE**

SELF-CARE

_____
_____
_____
_____
_____
_____
_____
_____

SELF-LOVE

_____
_____
_____
_____
_____
_____
_____
_____
_____

PROGRESS NOT PERFECTION

_____

_____

_____

_____

_____

_____

_____

_____

_____

_____

_____

_____

_____

_____

_____

_____

_____

_____

_____

_____

LIVE YOUR BEST LIFE

OWN-
ING
WHO
YOU
ARE

We're often taught, in one way or another, to build up walls. We do it as a way to protect ourselves, to shield ourselves from the unknown, from rejection, from failure. Strength, we're told, comes from knowledge.

But what if we've never been properly taught to ask the questions?

At the very core of "self-love" is vulnerability. And there's real power in it. In the "I don't knows." In asking for help when you need it. And most importantly, in being open with yourself and with others.

Self-love requires a look inward and doing the due diligence of asking those hard questions. It requires patience and work.

It also requires time. Let's start by creating some.

Important Reminders

They might seem obvious, but sometimes
these things just need to be said.

STAY ON THE CROOKED PATH—
those twists and turns are part of the journey.

DON'T BE AFRAID OF NO
or knowing your limits.

DON'T MAKE ASSUMPTIONS—

ask questions instead.

INTERACT WITH THE WORLD—

the world's better and brighter IRL.

BE ON TIME—

value your time and someone else's.

TO KNOW YOURSELF

is to love yourself.

Mind, Body, and Soul

DE-STRESS ON THE DAILY

Meditation can sometimes feel anxiety-inducing rather than calming. "How can I possibly sit still when I have about a thousand items on my to-do list and a million tabs open in my mind?"

It takes a conscious effort to relax our minds and find our peace, and it can really help recharge your brain and even increase your productivity. It's also a great way to check in with yourself and your body, giving it a brief moment to reset and focus.

Figure out what you're willing to commit to and then try to stick with it. Even if it's just ten minutes, the first step is trying.

FIND YOUR MANTRA

We all wake up on the wrong side of the bed sometimes. To shift your mind-set, create daily mantras—quick statements of positivity—that can help change the wrong side of the bed to the right side.

Daily mantras will help build concentration and focus, *and* uplift your mood. They can be recited out loud or mentally, especially in a difficult situation when you need to distract yourself from stress.

But don't just take our word for it! Try it yourself: Write down a few mantras and repeat them once or twice and see how that affects your mood.

_____

_____

_____

_____

_____

_____

_____

_____

_____

LEVEL UP

Being active is healthy—for both your physical health *and* your mental health.

And you don't have to be the captain of the soccer team to be considered an active person. You can join a dance class or ride your bike after school. Get in the habit of taking a morning walk before first period or join a sports league that's interesting to you.

If working out or playing a sport isn't appealing to you, find a way that you *do* enjoy moving. Are you interested in bird watching? Try going on a hike to search for birds. Are you interested in volunteering and recycling? Sign up for a beach cleanup. Are you interested in clearing your mind? Try swimming or walking around the neighborhood. Physical exercise doesn't have to mean being a part of an organized sport. *You* get to decide what works best for you.

So what makes you want to move? Write it down here, and move at your own pace.

_____

_____

_____

JOIN THE MOVEMENT

Signing up for a volunteer event can make a real-world impact on a cause that you care about. There are so many organizations out there supporting the LGBTQIA+ community, demanding equal pay, striving for a greener earth, donating books and clothes, and so much more. Look into volunteer events in your community if you're interested. Seeking out ways to give back will help you gain new experiences and insights, meet new people, and even build future career options.

SURVIVING THE SOCIAL SCENE

Life is a balancing act, but sometimes it can be hard to keep all the plates spinning at once. You have to juggle classes, homework, tests, jobs, crushes, family, and friends. It's a lot. And sometimes all of that pressure causes us to feel alone.

In those moments of stress, it's important to turn to the community around you. Having a group of trustworthy friends and family can be a huge factor in staying true to yourself. Remember that it's okay to lean on people when you need to. You are *not* a burden.

And if you're looking for people to talk to, explore the things that already bring you joy. Whether you are interested in video games, reading, cooking, or politics, look at your surroundings. More likely than not, there are others out there with your same interests. Above all, remember this too shall pass. It's about how you approach the balancing act that matters.

So what sparks joy for you?

_____

_____

_____

SOCIAL MEDIA

Social media can be amazing. You can curate your life in a unique way. You can create stunning photos and express your personality. You can connect with friends down the street or around the world. But social media isn't always amazing. Remember that it's important to be your own person. Commit to being authentic. Trust your instincts. Be careful with your personal information. Try to find the amazing parts of it, and if you discover that social media just isn't for you, that's okay, too. Forge your own path!

DATING

You're getting ready to go out with your crush on a date, and you're feeling all the butterflies. What if you sweat too much? What if you say the wrong thing? What if the closest thing you have to chemistry is your third-period class?

The thing about dating is that you'll never know until you try.

Here are a few things to remember when you're on your date:

- Don't be afraid to make your feelings known. Getting clarification is one of the healthiest things you can do for yourself.

- Make sure that you've actually had a conversation with your crush before asking them out. Actually get to know them and see if the banter flows!

- Show the person who you really are! Because the most attractive thing ever is someone being themselves.

○ Consent is key. Communicate with your date every step of the way. Because love, above all, is respect.

So don't be afraid to put yourself out there. Tell your crush you like them. Be intentional. Find new ways to be romantic. Be communicative. That way, you'll start to figure out what you like and what you don't, and ultimately build healthy and successful relationships.

The Tough Stuff

WE NEED TO TALK

Thinking of a conversation you've been putting off? Let's talk about it.

It can be really tricky and uncomfortable to have that one conversation you've been avoiding with someone. Maybe you've tried and it didn't go as planned. Maybe you fear that talking will only make the situation worse. Either way, you feel stuck.

An open line of communication is the only path forward, because oftentimes, the only way out is *through*. And in order to wade through the storm, prepare yourself by asking a few fundamental questions to get a better sense of the situation:

- What is your purpose for having the conversation?

- What do you hope to accomplish?

- What would be an ideal outcome?

- What assumptions are you making about this person's intentions?

- How have you contributed to the problem?

- How has the other person?

_____

_____

_____

_____

_____

_____

_____

_____

Once you've laid the groundwork, acknowledge their side of the story. If you see where they stand, you'll be able to productively advocate for yourself and find the best way forward.

COMING OUT

Sharing this huge part of who you are can be extremely freeing, but also terrifying. Your head is full of so many questions: Should I come out? If so, who do I tell? And when? What will they say? What if I'm not sure? What now?

The truth is that every coming-out story is different. Everyone's process is shaped by their comfort level, safety, and general readiness. If you are thinking about coming out, create your own terms and do what feels right for you.

- Get creative. Having a face-to-face talk is not the only way to come out. If that feels too hard, try writing a letter instead. That way, you'll have all the space you need to come out on your own terms, and it'll give your family and friends time to respond.

- Be willing to give people time to process and ask questions. It may come as a complete surprise to them. Surprise and shock don't always mean disapproval, though. They might need your support as much as you need theirs. If at first there's a hard response, it doesn't mean that'll be the response forever.

- Coming out is not a race. Choose one person who you trust—a friend, sibling, parent/guardian, or teacher—to share your news with. As soon as you've opened up to the first person, it might feel a little bit easier.

- Stay positive. It's easy to let your nerves get the best of you, but remember that coming out is part of living your most authentic life.

- Some coming-out experiences are harder than others. Assess what the pros, cons, and potential risks of coming out at that moment are and act accordingly. It's okay to wait till you're in a safer place. Above all, this moment is about you and your story . . . no one else's.

No matter who you are or what you like, coming out is an extremely normal and healthy part of your journey to self-love.

As Karamo says, this journey isn't about "coming out"—it's about "inviting them in." Give the power back to yourself to create your truth and your life. You're stronger and more resilient than you think. And don't let anyone tell you otherwise.

~~~~~~~~~

LGBTQIA+ RESOURCES

If you, a friend, or a loved one are part of the LGBTQIA+ community, check out these resources to learn more about how to get help or find someone to talk to:

ACT UP
www.actupny.com

A diverse, nonpartisan group of individuals committed to direct action to end the AIDS crisis

GLSEN
www.glsen.org

Formerly known as the Gay, Lesbian & Straight Education Network, GLSEN champions LGBT issues in K–12 education.

GSA NETWORK
www.gsanetwork.org

Helps LGBTQ+ students and straight allies
organize GSA (genders and sexualities alliance)
clubs to create safer schools

PFLAG
www.pflag.org

Parents, Families, and Friends of Lesbians and Gays

STONEWALL COMMUNITY FOUNDATION
www.stonewallfoundation.org

A community foundation for lesbian, gay, bisexual,
transgender, queer, and ally donors, volunteers,
and grant- and scholarship-seekers

THE TREVOR PROJECT
www.thetrevorproject.org

Provides information to LGBTQ+ youth through the
Trevor Support Center and TrevorChat features,
as well as a suicide prevention hotline

MENTAL HEALTH IS NOT A MYTH

We are all juggling so much—stress, anxiety, depression, grief—and all these emotions will start to add up. Our mental health has the power to affect every aspect of our lives. And it's time we spoke more openly about it.

Whether you're 12, 22, 52, or 100, mental health issues will be there. It's something everyone should be aware of because mental health has as much of an impact on our lives as our physical well-being does. So have check-ins with yourself. And reach out when it's too much.

MENTAL HEALTH RESOURCES

Your healthcare provider will have even more resources. But for now, here are some initial options for information and support:

- **National Suicide Prevention Lifeline:**
  www.suicidepreventionlifeline.org; 1-800-273-8255

- **Go Ask Alice:** www.goaskalice.columbia.edu

- **Crisis Line:** www.crisistextline.org; text TALK to
  741741 to text with a trained crisis counselor for
  free. Available 24/7

- **Reach Out:** www.au.reachout.com

- **Mindfulness for Teens:** www.mindfulnessforteens.com

- **SAMHSA's National Helpline:** www.samhsa.gov
  1-800-662-HELP (4357). Available 24/7

- **Love Is Respect's National Teen Dating
  Abuse Helpline:** www.loveisrespect.org
  1-866-331-9474; or text LOVEIS to 22522.
  Available 24/7

Also visit your:

- **Primary care provider**

- **Local psychiatric hospital**

- **Local walk-in clinic**

- **Local emergency department**

- **Local urgent care center**

home
design
&
your
safe
space

Your bedroom is so much more than a place to sleep. It is also a reflection of your personality and style. It should feel like *your* space, and more importantly, it should feel like a safe and secure space, a place where you can relax and recharge.

Reimagining your room doesn't have to be about buying new furniture or new pieces, either. Instead, small touches can add personality to help create the haven that you deserve.

As you brainstorm new ideas, remember that your bedroom is an expression of who you are. Design is very personal, so these are just tips that we hope will make you feel good in your room—no matter what else is going on.

It's sometimes helpful to do a slow rollout of your design vision, too. Clean up. Organize. Plan layout. Paint. Decorate. There are so many options in reimagining, so it's up to you if you want to start with one change or start with all the changes. It's also dependent on what you can afford to do, if you share a room and need to consider multiple styles, and how best to make your space, well, feel like *your* space. Rank the things that need to be done first so you can budget accordingly. There are little things that add big vibes!

SPRING CLEANING (BUT ALL YEAR ROUND)

We know, we know, you probably hear "clean your room" more times per week than you can count, but we're here to tell you: It really does help to have a clean and organized space. Getting rid of the clutter also makes it functional for you.

- **DECLUTTER:** If even the word "declutter" made you think "absolutely not," we get it! Try putting on your favorite music to help get you moving. Time will feel like it's moving faster if you're simultaneously jamming out. Then, go through your belongings and decide what you want to keep and what you're willing to get rid of.

> **PRO TIP:** *Check with your family before tossing, donating, or recycling anything. There might be some sentimental things they want to keep! You can just move it out of your space in that scenario . . . and into theirs.*

- **ORGANIZE:** Maximize any storage space you have! If you have bookshelves, hanging closet shelves, under-the-bed bins or totes, a storage bench, a bedside table, dresser drawers, etc., make the most of *every* inch of your room.

- **CLEAN:** This might feel like the worst part at the time . . . the dusting, making your bed, vacuuming, and laundry part of it all. But once it's done, hop on your just-made bed and breathe in. You'll feel calmer. Promise!

ROOM REMODEL

So what's on your room remodel vision board?

Rearranging your furniture to fit your space is one of the best ways to start creating something that is all yours! If you share a room with a sibling or inherited a room that doesn't exactly scream *you*, or if your room is small, don't worry. There are still ways to incorporate your own style. Remember, there's no right or wrong way for your space to be—it just needs to work for you and make you feel good every time you are in it.

Before you rearrange, map out your room by drawing your plan.

On the following page, decide where you'd want your furniture to maximize space and comfort. But also think about where you'd want your reading nook or your homework spot or your yoga mat or even your dance party space. No matter what your space is, be sure to have areas in your room where you can focus on things you love to do.

DECOR IDEAS FOR YOUR SPACE

Now that your room is decluttered and your furniture is where you want it, it's time to decorate! And while you may not be able to pick out your own furniture, bedding, or flooring, you *can* add details to make the space feel like your own. Adding these final details will let your personality shine through and also (hopefully!) make your room feel homey and unique. Our favorite part? It's always evolving. As your interests shift, so can the extra decoration adds.

If you're wary of a room overhaul, try taking little steps. Reposition your bed. Maybe you'll end up cultivating some good feng shui! Cover your wall with a tapestry. Add plants or a rug. If you inherited antique furniture that has to stay, find other areas you can add in your style: a funky lamp, wall art, or even accented curtains.

WALLS

Wake up your walls! One of the best ways to freshen up a room is to turn to the walls, and there are so many possibilities.

- You could paint an accent wall or even wallpaper one. Maybe you or a friend is an artist and you want to create your own piece of art or experiment with one wall as a geometric pattern? Or maybe you want to turn one of your walls into a chalkboard using special chalkboard paint? And don't forget about the fifth wall: the ceiling.

- When it comes to paint, white paint can go a long way to making a space feel brighter and lighter, but don't be afraid to experiment with bright, bold color, too. For example, yellow paint is known to communicate happiness, while blue paint is said to be calming.

- If you're already happy with the color of your room but still want to mix it up, look into adding wall decals, photos, or posters. A cork board or magnetic dry erase board can also be a great add for photos, reminders, or concert-ticket memories, along with becoming an added pop of color.

CURTAINS

They're functional *and* decorative . . . just the kind of decor we like!

- If you love sleeping in on the weekends, try adding dark curtains to keep the light out a bit longer. If you're an early bird, you can decorate with sheer curtains so the sunlight will wake you up in the morning.

ACCENT PIECES

It's always nice to have a statement piece in your room and that statement piece can be anything you want!

- If you don't already have something that feels like you, try looking into vintage furniture. Local garage sales and flea markets are often a treasure trove of unique pieces.

- If you're interested in an extra bit of creativity, you can reupholster an old chair or paint a dresser (an ombré pattern, perhaps?) and add some fun new knobs. Little touches go a long way in turning bargain finds into golden finds!

- A fun find that is also a surprising bedroom addition is a ladder! Lean a ladder against a wall and it soon becomes extra shelving, a blanket holder, or a place for all your extra books.

RUGS

An area rug is another way to revamp your room!

- If you want to create a hangout spot in your room, try adding a few throw pillows and a rug. A corner will work if space is a challenge!

BEDDING AND PILLOWS

Maybe *the* most important place in your bedroom? It's where you get all your best sleeping done, of course. Try to make it both comfy and cute.

- Adding a new bedding set will *instantly* upgrade your room. If you love your current bedding, though, switching out your blankets or pillows will add some good vibes.

LIGHTING

Don't let anyone dull your light, especially not in your bedroom.

- Regardless of your room's overall lighting (natural, fan light, lamps, etc.), consider where else you might need a light. Maybe at your desk for homework or on your nightstand for some before-bed reading.

- One of our favorite things to do is to also hang string lights above a headboard or reading nook to create special mood lighting. There'll always be something magical about a string of lights.

THAT DIY VIBE

There are always "do it yourself" projects that are inexpensive or free, too! By creating your own decor, you'll make your space feel even more personal. Get creative and have some fun deciding what you want to create. Here are some of our favorites to help inspire you.

PROJECT 1: *STRING ART*

If you're looking for an accent piece for above your bed or desk, look no further! Geometric shapes, an ombré effect, a monogrammed look, or a themed piece help give this '70s craft an up-to-date look. It's a low-cost way to add art to your walls, and it's something you can make unique to your style and the vibe you want for your space. All you'll need is a wood board, a hammer, nails, string, your imagination . . . and patience. And for complete honesty, the "stringing" of the art is kind of therapeutic—it feels like a win-win.

PROJECT 2: *PLANT HANGERS*

Plants like succulents need minimal maintenance and can really add a nice touch of color (and nature!) to your room. Make your own planters using a macramé technique so you can hang your new plant from the ceiling all year long. You basically need to tie knots (in varying techniques— completely up to you!) using hemp, jute, cotton cord, or fabric strips.

SKIN CARE

&

GROOMING

Grooming and skin care can play a big part in helping you feel great! Whether you have five or thirty minutes, grooming is something you can make work for your schedule. Try getting into a routine so it'll begin to feel like an essential first step of self-love. You'll soon start your day feeling like you can take on anything.

SKIN

Even five minutes in the morning and five minutes before bed can make a big difference. No matter what your schedule is, little actions add up.

THE SKIN YOU'RE IN

After washing your face, wait a bit and then take a look at yourself in the mirror . . . really get in there.

And then ask yourself: What type of skin do I have?

- **DRY:** *feels tight and might even have some flaky or rough patches*

- **OILY:** *feels shiny and greasy all over, but especially in your T-zone (forehead, nose, chin, and the area around the mouth)*

- **COMBINATION:** *will be oily in the T-zone, but with dryness in areas like the cheeks or jawline*

- **SENSITIVE:** *sometimes gets red, irritated, or itchy*

Then find the products that work best for you.

OILY

DRY

COMBINATION

SENSITIVE

1. CLEANSE

Cleansing twice a day (once in the morning and once at night) is key! Add a facial cleanser to your routine that can remove all that dirt. Look at the ingredients, too—to be sure they work for your skin type. A cleanser should leave your skin feeling clean, refreshed, and, most importantly, comfortable.

PRO TIP: *Warm water is essential to open pores.*

Some people find their skin feels better after air-drying it instead of patting it dry with a towel. Test out both and see what works for you! Rubbing your face dry with a towel is a no-go because it removes proteins, natural oils, and other important goodness from your face. Gotta keep that healthy barrier intact!

2. TONE

A facial toner is an extra step for cleaning your skin and will help remove excess oil and built-up dead skin cells. Toners also help restore the pH balance of your skin *and* tighten your pores. It's a win-win-win. Yasss balance!

PRO TIP: *You can use a cotton pad to apply toner or sprinkle it into your hands and tap directly onto skin. Either way, work outward on your face.*

3. MOISTURIZE

Just like your body needs hydration, so does your skin! Add a moisturizer as your final step to perk up your skin. Over time, it'll reduce fine lines and wrinkles, too. (It's worth it!)

For people with dry skin, a water-based serum will help keep your face moisturized all day. Whereas a person with oily or acne-prone skin would want to find a moisturizer that hydrates *and* absorbs.

PRO TIP: *Have hydration checks with yourself! You might need to reevaluate your moisturizer routine post-flight or seasonally!*

4. SUNSCREEN

Are you heading off to spring break, or summer vacation, or just hanging by the pool? Maybe you're going for a morning run or reading a book in the park? If you're doing *any* of these things, put sunscreen on. You'll thank yourself (and us!) when you're older.

PRO TIP: *Try zinc oxide sunscreen as a natural alternative to chemical sunscreens. It protects you from UVA/UVB rays that cause sunburns.*

5. FACE MASKS

A face mask as a special treat, at a sleepover with friends, or even before a big test can be a great way to show yourself some self-love and be healthy at the same time. There are face masks for pore cleansing, extra hydration, energizing, and more. But only leave them on for as long as the instructions say. Less is definitely more!

THE BENEFITS OF ESSENTIAL OILS

Stressed? Angsty? Have a headache? The fragrance of essential oils is an obvious perk and can act as a perfume or cologne, but oils can also enhance your mood, boost your confidence, and create the space you need to destress.

Here's a rundown of three essential oils that have the power to make you feel good. There are so many scents with so many different purposes. This is just a starting point! Make sure to use them safely. They can be too dangerous if misused but wonderful when used properly.

 LAVENDER OIL: perfect for stress relief

 PEPPERMINT OIL: super effective for headaches!

 SANDALWOOD OIL: will help you focus and calm nerves. Big test coming up? This'll do the trick. Can you believe?

ACNE COVER-UP TIPS

*What do you do if you get a pimple before the
Friday night football game? Or prom?
Or your first date with your crush?*

1. Less is more, and it's all about light layers! The more makeup you apply, the more attention you'll most likely draw to your pimple.

2. Try a concealer with salicylic acid, which'll help shrink the blemish *while* concealing it.

3. Dab your concealer with a sponge or small brush to help conceal all around the blemish.

4. If needed, use your finger to soften and blend the edges. This'll match the concealer to your face.

5. Set it with powder until it's matte all around.

6. Last but not least, take a breath! When it comes to imperfections, we're often our own worst critics. It probably looks and feels worse than it is. Go out and have fun! Root for the home team! Dance all night!

ANNOYING SKIN ISSUES

Even with a daily routine, you might find that your skin doesn't always cooperate the way you want it to . . . and that's okay. Acne, blackheads, and pimples are incredibly normal, and no one can escape them. But when they rear their heads, don't panic. Do your research. Ask questions. You'll see that you're not alone, and you'll find a skin-care routine that works perfectly for you. Because the skin you're in is exactly that—yours.

If you are struggling with breakouts, though, here are a few things you can do:

1. Use over-the-counter products. Cleansers and toners with ingredients like salicylic acid or benzoyl peroxide have anti-inflammatory properties that can help calm the redness and swelling that acne causes. In some cases, these ingredients can make acne worse, though. If after three to four weeks of use, you aren't seeing improvement or you're seeing intense drying or flaking, check with a dermatologist about what ingredients *will* help.

2. Tailor your diet by adding foods with omega-3 fatty acids (like salmon) and foods with antioxidants (like leafy greens and fruit). This can actually help clear up acne! Then try limiting foods like dairy or greasy fast foods, which may worsen acne by increasing hormone levels.

3. Manage your stress. Meditating (even for five minutes in the morning!), exercising, writing in a journal, asking for help, and talking things over with your parents or your friends are all great ways to relieve the stress of being pulled in a hundred different directions.

4. Don't over-exfoliate.

5. Regularly change and wash your towels *and* your pillowcases to get rid of bacteria.

6. Keep your phone screen clean! Think of how many times a day you touch your phone . . . that's a lot of germs (*ewwww*)!

7. Not all acne can be cured by self-management. If you're experiencing large bumps and nodules under your skin, ask your parents to take you to a dermatologist.

SKIN CARE AROUND THE WORLD

Do you want to hear a not-so-secret secret? When it comes to skin care, every country has its own popular beauty routine. No, seriously. It's true. Take a look at some of the best skin-care secrets from around the world and consider adopting some of them for yourself.

UNITED STATES:
witch hazel

FRANCE:
micellar water

ISRAEL:
mud from the Dead Sea

CHINA:
crushed pearls

SOUTH KOREA:
intensive skin cleaning and preservation

JAPAN:
silkworm cocoons

THAILAND:
lemongrass

INDONESIA:
turmeric

MYANMAR:
thanaka powder

SKIN CARE AROUND THE WORLD

JAPAN: If you have dead skin cells or clogged pores, silkworm cocoons are a popular method to remove that skin and unclog those pores. Thanks to the amino acids and proteins in the silk, it makes for a great natural exfoliator!

FRANCE: In France, it's not so much a secret beauty routine . . . it's a secret state of mind. The French focus on simplicity and consistency in their skin-care routine and have very little time for added fuss. Because of this mantra, they pick the best products and stick with them. One of them is micellar water. It's packed with H_2O and keeps skin hydrated all day long.

CHINA: Crushed pearls have been used in China for thousands of years to regenerate collagen and accelerate new skin growth. Maybe try out a mask with pearl extract for a little brightening before the first day of school!

ISRAEL: In Israel, mud from the Dead Sea is used for both pain relief and skin care because the mud is rich in magnesium, calcium, potassium, and iron. After a "soak" in the Dead Sea, your skin will feel noticeably softer!

UNITED STATES: Witch hazel is a plant with powerful medicinal properties. Because of that, it can be used for so many things: acne, burns, scalp sensitivity, inflammation, insect bites, itching, and more!

PRO TIP: *Use it after cleansing as a toner.*

THAILAND: Lemongrass can be used to detox the skin! The wonderful aroma doesn't hurt, either. Try a hand or body cream to calm your nerves while moisturizing your skin.

MYANMAR: Thanaka powder comes from the bark and roots of thanaka trees in Myanmar and is one of the oldest Burmese beauty secrets! If you mix it with water or honey, it creates a mask that can help acne.

INDONESIA: Turmeric is incorporated into skin-care routines here. It has powerful anti-inflammatory properties and can give you absolutely glowing skin.

SOUTH KOREA: Intensive skin cleaning and preservation is the name of the game! South Korea also happens to be one of the best beauty innovators in the world. No big deal! They are famous for their seven- or sometimes ten-step skin-care routines, BB creams, sheet masks, and more.

MAKEUP

You're beautiful. We don't say that to ourselves enough, but honestly, we should start.

Let's do it now. Find a moment to remind yourself of how beautiful you are. Because at the end of the day, how you own who you are and who you want to be is what's important.

The same idea is true about makeup. There are a million ways up the makeup mountain. But it's up to you to figure out how—or if—you want to get there. Makeup has no gender, and experimenting with different looks is one way to find what makes you feel great.

Whether it's a little concealer to cover a pimple, a full foundation moment, some green stick for red skin/ rosacea, or a dramatic cat eye, you have the power to pick what you want.

FINDING YOUR EVERYDAY LOOK

Finding your everyday look is not about trends. It's not about looking like someone that is not you or hiding something. It's about knowing what you feel comfortable with, how you'd like to present yourself, and above all, figuring out your essentials.

What are some beauty products you absolutely can't live without? Write down your Top Five here.

1. _____

2. _____

3. _____

4. _____

5. _____

THE CONCEALER TRIANGLE

Step aside, Illuminati—you have nothing on the concealer triangle. No, seriously.

The best way to apply concealer is to draw a triangle with the base under your eye and the point toward your cheek. This shape not only conceals dark circles, it also lifts your face and gives it a glow. Sometimes this takes a little practice, but always blend more, not less.

FINDING YOUR
SPECIAL OCCASION LOOK

Whether it's date night, prom, or a night on the town with your crew, finding a beauty look for a special occasion can sometimes be stressful. Option paralysis is definitely a thing; don't let anyone tell you otherwise.

But we can absolutely find ways to combat it. The goal of a special occasion look is to find a style that makes you feel like you . . . but with that extra special "I've got this! I can do this! I'm going to crush it!" energy. It could be a winged eyeliner. It could be matte orange-red lipstick. It could be a blush and bronzer combo. It could be going makeup-free. Whatever it ends up being, make sure it's you. Because that's what really matters.

At the end of the day, it's all about knowing your boundaries and knowing what makes *you* feel cute. Because confidence is the most important component in channeling your inner gorgeousness.

HIGHLIGHT YOUR LIFE

A little bit of highlighter can go a long way. Whether it's a powder, liquid, cream, or stick, highlighter is a face makeup that creates the illusion of brightness and accentuates the parts of you and your face that you really want to shine. Literally.

When using highlighter, focus on the bridge of the nose, diagonally down the cheekbones, under the brow bone, and on the Cupid's bow to give you a glow and make you look (and feel!) more awake.

Lastly, for those of us with facial hair, try using highlighter or illuminator cream just above your brow line to accentuate your cheekbones. Make sure to blend, blend, and blend some more to achieve a more natural glow!

HAIR

Let's be real, hair is never just hair. To some it's a means of self-expression. To others, the ultimate form of self-care. Your hair says something about you. So why shouldn't you treat it with love?

It's time to embrace all the hair that you have—from your eyebrows to your chest hair to the beautiful mop on your head. And as with any aspect of your life, you need to be in constant conversation with your hair in order to really understand it.

DID YOU KNOW YOUR HAIR HAS A TYPE?

Hair is so personal. That feels like such an obvious thing to say, but it *needs* to be said. We've all been told that only certain haircuts match certain face shapes. Whether you have an oblong, oval, diamond, round, triangular, or square face, there is a recommended cut for you, and that's the only factor here. Right?

Wrong! There's so much more to it! It's also about hair density and texture, which often inform the style and length of your hair, and your hair-care routine.

Finding out what texture you have is the first step to decoding your hair. You can even have more than one type of texture; you can have a combination of two or three!

THE RIGHT
STYLIST FOR YOU

It all starts with finding your stylist. Talk to your friends or do your research online to find a barber, stylist, or hairdresser in your neighborhood who specializes in the kind of cut you want *and* is within your price range. Above all, look for someone who asks questions. A good stylist will want to find out exactly what you like about your hair, what changes you're looking to make, and the overall look you're trying to go for. Open communication makes for a great haircut.

SPICE UP
LENGTHY LOCKS

If you're rocking longer locks, there's so many gorgeous looks that you can experiment with. Braid crowns? Regal. Sleek, long, and shiny? Chic. Loose beach waves? . . . Who gave you permission? No matter the look you want to try, remember to hydrate. Try a coconut honey mask or hydrating serum to keep your mane bouncy and healthy. You'll be unstoppable!

SHORT HAIR, DON'T CARE

Anyone can rock a short hairstyle. With the right cut, it can highlight all the beautiful features of your face. Plus, if your hair is on the thinner side, short hair can give you volume, body, and the illusion of thickness.

The most important thing about a short haircut is maintenance. Short hair appears to grow out faster and lose shape more rapidly, requiring more frequent visits to the salon. Then there's the products. Try texturizing spray, pomades, hair oils, or wax to create the edgy, sleek look of your dreams.

And if you're looking for a fade to show off your unique style? Well, the possibilities are basically endless. An undercut, a temp, a taper, a high top, a mid-fade . . . the list goes on and on. Plus! A fade can be tailored to appear subtle or striking, classic or modern *and* works on different hair types. It all depends on what you're looking for. How cool is that?

SHOULDER-LENGTH
HAIR FOR ALL!

The rules of hair care, of course, are meant to change and develop over time, but there are a few that feel universal: shoulder-length hair looks good on everyone. Long hair can make a long face appear longer. Short hair can make a round face appear rounder. But shoulder-length hair can create the right amount of volume and bounce you want without going over the top.

ABOVE ALL,
EXPERIMENT!

One of the most fun ways to show a little personality is to add some color to your hair. Whether you're after a bright purple updo or just subtle blond highlights, coloring your hair can be a huge complement to your overall look.

That said, it does require a bit of upkeep. If you decide to experiment with color, be sure to find a color-friendly shampoo and conditioner that will help moisturize and slow down the fade-out process. Consider a hot-oil treatment, or even a leave-in cream product to restore moisture to your hair, to keep it looking healthy and fresh.

EMBRACE YOUR BODY HAIR

It's time we have an open conversation about body hair.

We are taught to believe that having little body hair is more feminine and more body hair is more masculine. But here's the thing: No matter what your genetics gift you, rock what you want to rock, not what the world says you should.

It's time we make our own standards of beauty. Your body hair is what you make of it. And with the right regimen and products, you can learn how to take care of it more easily, too.

PEACH FUZZ, BEARDS, AND MUSTACHES, OH MY!

If you're not that into peach fuzz, there are certain things you can do to get rid of it. You can just keep it simple and use a delicate shaving oil or cream to shave it off.

As you get older and the beard starts, though, you have more options. You can shave your face or you can embrace your facial hair. It can sometimes be a game changer in your style!

Beard grooming is an art form, and here are some tips to keep in mind as you move through your beard journey:

- If you're thinking of experimenting with facial hair, set your razor down for four weeks and see where that takes you! Within a month, you can pretty much figure out what kind of beard results you'd get—and how to treat it.

- If you're past the four-week test and you want to keep your facial hair, here are some extra tips:

- *Use a beard trimmer to keep your facial hair looking fresh and clean. It's important to maintain the shape of your beard if you're growing it out, and regularly trim the hair to keep it healthy.*

- *You can also use beard oil during your morning routine to maintain moisture in your facial hair and on your skin. This will keep your beard soft instead of coarse and scratchy! Plus, that itchiness that comes with stubble? It'll be less intense thanks to a good moisturizer.*

- *When crafting your facial hair game, make sure you match it to whatever you're sporting on top of your head. If you have a skin fade, you'll want an equal fade with your sideburns. If your hair is a little tousled, try pairing it with a patchy (but always trimmed) beard.*

You can also experiment with different facial hair! A handlebar mustache or a five o'clock shadow? Why not! As you grow and evolve, your tastes will change and you may want to try different facial hair styles.

SAY "NO, THANKS" TO RAZOR BURN

If you're new to shaving, you'll need two things: shaving cream and a sharp, clean razor blade. Shaving with a dull razor will pull on your hair instead of cutting it.

But wait. Did you read that and think, "Wow, this is already intimidating"? Don't worry! You've got this! And if you feel like you don't, ask for help. Communication is key . . . even when it comes to razor burn.

So what's next? Map out which way your hair grows, and shave *with* the grain to avoid razor burn, irritation, or ingrown hairs.

Now here we go! Splash some warm water on your skin to open up the hair follicles. Apply a shaving cream or gel. Shave. Wash your face with a cleanser. Then apply aftershave or moisturizer to help close your pores and prevent skin irritation.

Remember that your facial hair is about how you want to present yourself. Pick a look and try it. You can always change it. Learn from detours. As with any leap you take, you might end up somewhere amazing!

Style is substance.

It's not about being the trendiest person in the room or about having the fanciest, most expensive clothing. Rather, it's about feeling *good* in the way you carry yourself and wear your clothes. Your style is unique and specific to you, not to what's on the 'gram.

Style isn't stagnant, either . . . it evolves over time. You may one day look back at pictures of yourself from years ago and question, "What was I thinking?" But that's all part of the process. Embrace your previous style choices because it's part of the fabric of who you are!

And honestly, your style will change depending on where you're going in each moment. Is it date night? Is it your best friend's birthday party? Is it school after you stayed up late working on your English paper? Is it your after-school job? Dress for where you're going and what feels right for that.

Lastly, style isn't about money. It can also come from your favorite thrift stores, flea markets, or your friend's silk-screening Etsy shop. You don't need to spend a lot of money to show off your style! Try to avoid feeling the pressure to look like everyone else. Your style is a great way to show the world what you're all about!

THE WARDROBE ESSENTIALS

Find the essential pieces of clothing that make you feel your best and then mix them up! As your tastes, interests, and style change over time, these are some key pieces that will be the foundation of every wardrobe, no matter what your style evolves to.

GOOD-VIBES JEANS:
jeans that accentuate all the right "ass-ets"

FEELS-LIKE-A-HUG SWEATERS:
for the days when all you need is a hug

BEST-FIT TEES:

from a simple white T-shirt to your favorite band
merch (ahem, the Strokes!), your best-fit tees
bring some flare to your wardrobe

COMFORT SHIRTS:

the ones that make you feel secure for
your big test or presentation

THE POWER JACKET:
a blazer or jacket that
makes you feel like a boss

LITTLE BLACK DRESS:
for when you want
to be overdressed or
underdressed, it's a
classic for a reason

CRUSH-THE-DAY FOOTWEAR:
so you can run toward any problem with full force

**SOLID PAIR OF
SWEATPANTS:**

perfect for those rainy days
when all you need is a good
book and some tunes

**GO-TO GOING-OUT
PANTS:**

to unleash your inner
rock star

THIS-IS-ME UNDERWEAR:

you know the ones

STYLING TIPS & TRICKS

Overall, though, what's most important when it comes to style is to dress for *your* body and what feels good on *you*. You don't have to dress for someone else's standards, and you don't have to mimic every trend.

NEXT-LEVEL LAYERING

Layering is all about experimentation. It takes time and practice to figure out what colors not only complement your skin but also work well together. Follow these simple tips to learn more about the art of layering:

- **COLOR CONSIDERATION:** There are great color combos for every season that can really elevate your look. Remember: a warm palette energizes your look, cooler colors subdue it, and neutral tones provide breathers in between. Layering works best when you keep to one or two colors families. Is it a delicate pale pink and gray? Yes, please. A tan with a burgundy? No problem. A navy blue with white? How chic! Play with color by placing the articles of clothing together in front of you to see what works best. It's kind of exciting to see what a kaleidoscope of colors could bring!

- **MAKE A STATEMENT:** Choose one statement piece, whether it's a striped tee, patterned pants, or bold kicks, and pair it with neutral tones to really give it the spotlight it deserves!

- **MIX AND MATCH TEXTURES:** Denim, chambray, velvet, metallic, lace, silk, wool—there are so many different textures to choose from! And when you pair them, they give dimension to your outfit. If you want to experiment with textures in one look, stick with one color family so you don't overwhelm the eye. If color is more the name of your game, be strategic with your fabrics.

PROPORTION PLAY

Here's the secret that no one ever tells you: Size and numbers don't really matter.

When it comes to layering and dressing for your body, *proportions* are everything. Your body can inform the type of clothes that you want to wear. You just need to know how to properly play with the "lines" clothes make, and then bend them to best suit your body.

Most of us know ye olde tale that horizontal stripes widen while vertical lines elongate, but these lines contain multitudes. The biggest mistake you can make is to cut your body in half at the hips. Instead, think about ways to visually break from that structure and let the eye travel.

Another factor that must be paid attention to is *volume*. Is it a friend or a foe? If two pieces are cut equally wide, it will make you look a bit boxy. A good way to remedy this is to play with opposites. For example, if you wear something looser fitting on your upper body, wear something more fitted on the bottom. This will create movement in your outfit!

Then, ask yourself: "Am I wearing this or is it wearing me?" Don't let it be the latter. Clothes are supposed to complement your look, never upstage or suffocate. Everything from the hemline of a skirt to the sleeve length of a sweater can give the little push your outfit needs to take it from drab to fab.

SUPER PRO TIP:
The French Tuck:
So simple and yet so foolproof! The French tuck— semi-tucking your shirt into your pants—gives your outfit both length and movement. Try it with your favorite blouse or sweater to add balance and elegance to your silhouette.

DETAILS, DETAILS, DETAILS

Even the most basic outfits transform with the right accessories. Shoes, bags, and jewelry are just a few options that you can choose from. The opportunities to accessorize your outfit (and your life!) are endless.

- **STATEMENT JEWELRY:** Jewelry can add a little something extra to an outfit. Experiment with long necklaces to give the illusion of elongating your body, or large earrings to bring more attention to your face.

- **KEEP IT FUNKY:** The more basic or neutral your outfit is, the more you can play with the details. Small accessories can really pop!

- **GLASSES:** The right pair of glasses can add a pop of personality to your outfit. But with so many different types of frames, how do you choose the right pair? It's all about the face shape. Choose glasses (and sunglasses!) that are the opposite of your face shape.

THE FORMAL OCCASION

In addition to the wardrobe staples filling your closet, it's also a good idea to have some formal options for different events, like homecoming dances, prom, and graduation. It's okay to even be a little extra at birthday parties and any big event you have coming up.

These events are the perfect opportunity to showcase your personal style and play up your look. Whether you're going for a suave suit, a glamorous gown, or a sexy minidress, you can make a statement with the right outfit and accessories. It's all about finding the right items (and the right tailor!) to create what works for you, your style, and your body.

SUITS

● If you're wearing a suit, try cropped pants. Then add some shoes with no-show socks to reveal a little ankle skin, or you can wear fun print or patterned socks. Either of these can show off your personality and set your outfit apart.

- Play with different shirt options, including solids and patterns. Generally, you will want to wear a solid shirt if your suit has a pattern or stripes. If your suit is solid, you can wear a plaid, striped, or printed shirt under the jacket for a put-together look. You can also wear a tie or bow tie to add a layer of fun!

DRESSES

- Bring some smiley energy to your night with an outfit starring you and one of the brightest-colored dresses you can find!

- If you're looking for something fun and flirty, try a look full of sparkles and sequins. You can even add sparkly jewelry for a glitzy glam effect.

- Maybe mix in a statement shoe to give a punch of punk rock and edge to your formal wear.

ACCESSORIES

- Accessories like a necklace, the right dress shoes, or a pocket square are a great way to showcase your personality and complete your look. Experiment with different options and find a combination that you love!

Style is a unique form of expression, and finding what works for you can be a fun, spontaneous, and inherently social experience. It is also deeply personal. The way that you find your style is by experimenting, trying *lots* of stuff on, and evolving. It's all about the journey—and if you do what makes you feel good, above all else, the world will see it, too.

HOW TO ROCK THE DANCE FLOOR (EVEN IF YOU HAVE TWO LEFT FEET)

First, try not to let fear keep you from getting on the dance floor and busting your moves. Confidence makes you a better dancer!

Second, don't do anything that makes you feel uncomfortable.

Third, dance breaks are real. Grab some punch. Head to the bleachers. Wait for a slow song. It's *your* dance, and you get to decide how it goes!

If you're interested in food, offer to help your parents by going to the grocery store together and learning how to make some of your favorite meals. Take the opportunity to discover new foods and cuisines. Developing a healthy relationship and interest in food goes a long way toward getting rid of that intimidation factor. Plus, it's a great way to help your family out, explore something that may become a passion, and have fun with your friends. Major bonus: It's an awesome way to have some influence on what you eat every day.

FILL YOUR PLATE WITH FOOD FROM AROUND THE WORLD

A great thing about food is that you can always try new things . . . especially new cuisines from around the world! Be open-minded, because the more types of food (and food experiences!) you try, the more you will find that you like.

- **ITALY:** Italian is a popular cuisine because its most famous dishes are built around pasta, pizza, gnocchi, risotto, and . . . gelato! Go beyond the basics you already know and love, and experiment with different vegetables or meats to begin exploring flavor. If you're up for a cooking challenge, try something like chicken cacciatore.

- **CHINA:** Many countries have their own version of the dumpling, but Chinese dumplings are best known. They can be steamed, boiled, or pan-fried, and made with different shapes and fillings, but no matter how they're made, there is no doubt they are delicious. Try making them with your family for dinner.

- **SPAIN:** Do you like shrimp? How about lobster? Mussels? Squid? You like all of these things? Well then mix them together, add some rice, and you'll be eating paella. It's a traditional Spanish dish, and it doesn't hurt that it's absolutely delicious.

- **JAPAN:** Sushi is particularly fun to make since many of the ingredients, like cucumbers, carrots, avocados, etc., are already finger foods. Wrap sushi with your friends at your next sleepover!

- **CANADA:** Poutine is gravy, french fries, and cheese curds—what's not to love? Some restaurants have over one hundred variations to choose from, with all sorts of toppings. Bacon? Yes. Sweet potato? Yes. Avocado? Yes, yes, yes!

- **FRANCE:** Take an imaginary trip to Paris and whip up a batch of crepes, which are basically very yummy, super-thin, filled pancakes. You can make sweet or savory variations. Our favorites are ham and cheese, and strawberries with sugar. There's really no wrong filling, so experiment with your favorites for your next Paris-themed movie night.

● **VIETNAM:** The classic noodle soup dish known as pho is one of the tastiest and comfiest foods we've ever tried. It is deceptively simple and has complex flavors that are a perfect treat for a night out with your friends or a stay-in rainy afternoon. Or try the Vietnamese sandwich banh mi. Filled with amazing savory ingredients, it has all the components to be one of the best sandwiches ever. That's right . . . ever!

These examples are just the tip of the iceberg, too! There are so many more countries and foods to explore. So why not get out a map or a globe, pick a random spot, and then try a cuisine from that place.

DIETS

In addition to the myriad of cuisines to choose from, there are also various "diets" ranging from plant based (no meat or seafood) to omnivorous (a balance of all types of food). Some people experiment with eliminating certain food groups for health concerns (like gluten or dairy allergies) and sometimes just for overall health or preference.

If you're feeling up for a challenge, try one of these for a day or even a full week to see how incorporating or eliminating certain foods changes how you experiment with food and how you feel. There's no one-size-fits-all diet, though, so try what you like best and find the balance that works for you.

OMNIVORE: Eat a balance of plant- and meat-based foods. Fruits and vegetables, along with dairy, grains, and meats, like chicken, beef, pork, turkey, and seafood, are all perfect for meal planning on this diet.

PESCATARIAN: Eat all the fruits and veggies you want, as well as dairy and seafood. Pescatarians do *not* eat any meat from land animals, though, so this means no beef, poultry, pork, etc.

VEGETARIAN: Eat plant-based foods, grains, and dairy, but eliminate any type of meat, including seafood. Eggs and cheese are optional!

VEGAN: Completely plant based. Eliminate any type of meat or product that comes from animals, which includes dairy and cheese.

TIME TO COOK!

Here are some different recipes you can use for your school lunch, snack time, or those nights when you help cook dinner.

If these aren't calling you to the kitchen, do some research and find different recipes that use *your* favorite ingredients. The joy of cooking is all about experimenting and trying new things!

If you're new to using the oven or stovetop to cook, though, please ask an adult for help. They can teach you the basics, and you can teach them a new recipe.

CHICKEN SALAD MEAL

. . . .

INGREDIENTS

FOR THE CHICKEN SALAD

- 1 avocado (optional)
- 1½ cups chopped celery
- 1 cup mayonnaise
- 2 teaspoons sugar
- 2 teaspoons sweet relish *or*
  2 teaspoons lemon juice
- 3 boneless chicken breasts, cooked and
  shredded

FOR THE SANDWICH

- 1 whole wheat English muffin or wrap
- 1 handful lettuce or sunflower sprouts
- 2 slices tomato

DIRECTIONS

1. In a bowl, mix all the salad ingredients together until the chicken is thoroughly coated with the mayonnaise.

2. Serve your chicken salad on top of a bed of lettuce without any bread, or split on top of an English muffin with tomato slices and sunflower sprouts or lettuce. If you don't want to use an English muffin, you can use a wrap instead.

BREAKFAST EGG CUPS

• • • • • • • • • • • • • • • •

INGREDIENTS

- 12 eggs

- 2 tablespoons chopped onion

- A pinch of salt and pepper

- Pick one of the following toppings, or combine and come up with your own creation:

    - *Spinach (roughly chopped), cherry tomatoes (halved), shredded mozzarella*

    - *Chopped bacon or ham and shredded cheddar cheese*

    - *Sliced mushrooms and diced bell peppers*

PRO TIP: *This recipe is perfect for cooking ahead of time! Wrap each cup up individually in plastic wrap before putting them in the freezer. They'll last all week for a quick grab-and-go breakfast treat. Just reheat in the microwave for about 20 seconds.*

DIRECTIONS

1. Preheat the oven to 350 degrees Fahrenheit.

2. Spray a nonstick muffin or cupcake pan with a light coating of cooking spray or line each with paper liners.

3. Whisk the eggs together with the onion, salt, and pepper.

4. Pour the egg mixture evenly into the muffin or cupcake pan, filling each cup about ¾ full.

5. Top with your favorite ingredients.

6. Bake for 20 minutes and enjoy!

CUCUMBER TUNA BITES

• • • • • • • • • • • • • • •

INGREDIENTS

FOR THE TUNA SALAD

- 1 can tuna, drained
- 2 tablespoons chopped celery
- 1 tablespoon diced red onion
- ¼ cup mayonnaise
- A pinch of salt and pepper

FOR THE BITES

- 2 cucumbers, peeled

DIRECTIONS

1. Combine the tuna, celery, red onion, mayonnaise, and salt and pepper in a bowl. Mix well!

2. Slice the cucumbers into roughly ½- to ¾-inch pieces. Smear tuna on the cucumber pieces.

3. Enjoy!

THE ULTIMATE GRILLED CHEESE

. . . .

INGREDIENTS

- 2 slices of your favorite bread, buttered
- 2 slices of your favorite cheese

OPTIONAL ADD-INS

- 2 bacon slices
- ½ avocado
- 2 tomato slices
- Sliced mushrooms

PRO TIP: *Feel free to play here! You can add prosciutto as your meat or go full vegetarian, too.*

DIRECTIONS

1. In a skillet over medium heat, place one slice bread, butter-side down. Toast that side 4–5 minutes while you add on the goodies!

2. Add one slice of your favorite cheese first, then the rest of your ingredients (bacon, avocado, tomato, mushrooms, or whatever you like). Top with the second slice of cheese.

3. Place the second slice of bread on top, butter-side up.

4. Flip over and cook another 4–5 minutes or until lightly browned and the cheese has melted.

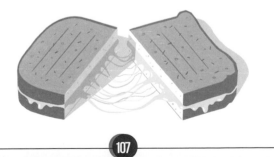

MASON JAR SALAD

•••••••••••••••

INGREDIENTS

- Dressing: your choice!

- Vegetables: your choice!

- Cheese: your choice!

- Protein: your choice!

- Fruits and nuts: your choice!

- Leafy greens: your choice!

- Croutons: you guessed it . . . also your choice!

DIRECTIONS

1. When it comes to a mason jar salad, it's all about how you layer your ingredients in the jar! Start with the dressing, then your veggies, then your cheese and/or protein, fruits, or even nuts if you want them, then leafy greens and croutons on top!

2. When you're ready to eat, unscrew the top, dump all ingredients into a bowl, and dig in.

CHARCUTERIE PLATTER

. . . .

INGREDIENTS

- Meat: salami, pepperoni, prosciutto, etc.

- Cheese: Brie, Gouda, mozzarella, blue cheese, etc.

- Fruit or nuts: grapes, berries, almonds, etc.

- Jams, mustards, or honeys

- Crackers

DIRECTIONS

1. This is your ultimate experiment-and-have-fun snack! Choose your own favorites, adventure with something new, and enjoy all the sweet and savory goodness this plate has to offer. Choose one or two from each category on the ingredients list and place on a shareable plate. It's perfect for a friends' night in.

BAKED SWEET POTATO FRIES

· · · · · · · · · · · · · · · · · ·

INGREDIENTS

- 2 large sweet potatoes, peeled and cut into strips about ½ inch wide and thick

- 2 tablespoons olive oil

- Salt and pepper

DIRECTIONS

1. Preheat the oven to 425 degrees Fahrenheit.

2. Line a baking sheet with parchment paper so the fries don't get stuck when they're done (and when you're ready to munch).

3. Toss the potato strips with olive oil till they're evenly coated. Sprinkle with salt and pepper (or any other seasonings you may like—garlic powder, paprika, etc.!).

4. Arrange your fries on the baking sheet in a single layer and don't overcrowd them.

5. Bake for 20 minutes, then flip the fries so they cook on all sides.

6. Bake for another 10 minutes or until the fries are golden brown. Keep an eye on them, as they can turn from crisp to burnt very quickly.

BAKED KALE CHIPS

•••••••••••••••

INGREDIENTS

- 1 large bundle kale
- 2 tablespoons olive oil
- Seasonings: salt, chili powder, other— the choice is yours!

DIRECTIONS

1. Preheat the oven to 275 degrees Fahrenheit.

2. Rinse and dry the kale, then tear into small pieces. Discard the large stems!

3. Put the kale into a large mixing bowl and add the oil and seasonings. Toss to combine. You can even use your hands to really get it mixed up.

4. Spread the kale on a baking sheet. Try to keep the pieces from touching if possible. This'll get them *extra* crispy. You can even use two baking sheets if needed.

5. Bake for 15 minutes and then move the kale around a little on the pan so it cooks evenly. Be careful here! Don't burn yourself on the oven or baking pan. It should take another 10 minutes or so, but keep an eye on it.

6. Remove from the oven, cool, and eat!

PUT YOUR CHEF'S HAT ON

What are your favorite recipes to make?

RECIPE NAME:

_____

FROM THE KITCHEN OF:

_____

INGREDIENTS:

_____ _____

_____ _____

_____ _____

_____ _____

_____ _____

DIRECTIONS:

_____

_____

_____

_____

_____

_____

_____

RECIPE NAME:

_____

FROM THE KITCHEN OF:

_____

INGREDIENTS:

_____   _____

_____   _____

_____   _____

_____   _____

_____   _____

DIRECTIONS:

_____

_____

_____

_____

_____

_____

_____

RECIPE NAME:

_____

FROM THE KITCHEN OF:

_____

INGREDIENTS:

_____   _____

_____   _____

_____   _____

_____   _____

_____   _____

DIRECTIONS:

_____

_____

_____

_____

_____

_____

_____

RECIPE NAME:

_____

FROM THE KITCHEN OF:

_____

INGREDIENTS:

_____ _____

_____ _____

_____ _____

_____ _____

_____ _____

DIRECTIONS:

_____

_____

_____

_____

_____

_____

_____

_____

QUICK TIPS & TRICKS

1. Eat breakfast. No, really. Everyone says it's the most important meal of the day. And they're not wrong. It is. It'll help start you off on the right foot by kick-starting your metabolism and giving your body the fuel it needs to power your muscles and brain.

2. Drink *a lot* of water. Your body needs eight glasses a day, so try your best to get there. If you're asking why . . . it delivers oxygen to your body, it boosts skin health, it flushes body waste (you asked!), and it regulates your body temperature. Just to mention a few. So carry a water bottle with you so it's on the top of your mind all day. You can even experiment and try water infused with fruit flavors like strawberry, apple, or lemon.

3. If you do want or crave fast food, it's okay once in a while. Just choose wisely.

4. Keep healthy snacks on hand for munching. Some of our favorites: fresh fruit (try washing and cutting it up on Sunday and putting it in a bowl in the fridge so you can just grab a helping of it and go), pretzels, mixed nuts, granola bars, yogurt, etc.

PRO TIP: *Not all granola bars are created equal. Check to see if they have fiber and protein—that's the good stuff! And try to find a bar with less than eight grams of sugar. Otherwise, you might find yourself in a sugar crash later in the day.*

HOST WITH THE MOST!

As Antoni says, "There should be no rules at your dinner party except for people to eat a lot and enjoy a long night."

Using food is the perfect way to connect with people. Even if your comfort zone isn't in the kitchen, that's okay! Take the opportunity that comes with cooking and eating to socialize and showcase your interests. Themed parties often provide a great setting to try out new recipes and ideas. So put on your hosting shoes, and let's cook!

KARAOKE

Singing is the main attraction at a karaoke party, so make sure you have water on hand! But you can also have small snacks for guests to munch on, like a fruit salad, mixed nuts, or even some bite-size desserts.

HALLOWEEN

Besides eating *all* the candy, there are some other tricks you can use to make the perfect holiday treats. Trick number one: After carving your pumpkins, save the seeds! Wash them thoroughly and then toss them with melted butter. Next up: Choose your seasoning. Either cinnamon or salt added to the seeds will impress even your jack-o'-lantern. Cook on a baking sheet for 45 minutes (stirring a few times) at 300 degrees Fahrenheit.

THE SUPER BOWL

Dips, dips, and more dips! We're talking nacho dip, vegetable dip, bean dip, cheese dip, pizza dip, all the dip! As each team heads down to touchdown territory, you'll be heading down for the next potato or pita chip. It's the perfect Sunday scenario.

MOVIE NIGHT

Pick your favorite movie and then theme the night around it! Try out a s'mores dip! Or a fruit wand! If it's a superhero movie, use fruit and marshmallows to make a superhero's shield, or dye your Rice Krispies treats the color of the superhero's cape.

SLEEPOVER

One of the best parts of a sleepover is hanging out with your friends. DIY masks? Check yes. Listening to new music? Always! Themed late-night menu? We're ready. Why not try a popcorn bar? Popcorn is a sleepover necessity, but have each friend pick their own toppings: salt, butter, cinnamon, chili powder, caramel sauce, chocolate sauce? The possibilities are endless.

MURDER MYSTERY

Make Nancy Drew and the Hardy Boys proud by hosting your very own murder mystery party. You can serve carrot fingers (carrots dipped in hummus to look like nails—looks gross, but it's delicious and spooky) or mummy dogs (dough wrapped around hot dogs to look like mummies).

GAME NIGHT

It's a good idea to have some no-mess snacks on hand. If you're solving a murder in the billiard room or about to win in The Game of Life, you want to be able to concentrate and eat with one hand. Look into soft pretzel bites, skewers, or even mini quiches.

NEW YEAR'S EVE

The countdown is officially on. 10 . . . 9 . . . 8 . . . you're starting to think of your goals for the new year . . . 7 . . .

6 . . . 5 . . . and recapping the last year, remembering how you grew and learned and changed . . . 4 . . . 3 . . . 2 . . . 1! And also remembering all the awesome food you learned how to make, like tacos and salads and pie.

~~~~~~~~~~

OLYMPICS

It's always fun to get your friends and family together to watch the Olympics and cheer for your country. It's maybe even *more* fun to theme your food for the event. Maybe try making Olympic ring pizzas? Or even cookies shaped and decorated like medals? If the Olympics are hosted in a city or country that is famous for a certain dish, add it to the list!

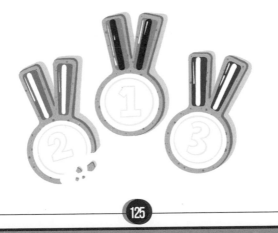

SOME PARTING WORDS

The road to self-love is never as clear as you imagine it to be. Like, *never*. There'll always be detours and forks in the road. But it's how you choose to navigate through them that often makes all the difference.

However you choose to use this book, know that the steps that you take to changing your life don't have to be cosmically life-altering. They can be as small as trying a new makeup look, a new hairstyle, or a new recipe. They can be as fun and creative as reimagining your room. They can be as simple as reciting words of positivity to yourself. You don't have to do it all at once. Try things out. Explore and see where your life takes you.

Above all, be true to yourself. Ask questions. Know that you are capable of receiving and giving love.

And just breathe. The rest will follow.

Acknowledgments

David Collins, Rob Eric, and Michael Williams, the executive producers of *Queer Eye*, would like to thank . . .

The Fab Five for their message of self-love and self-acceptance.

Illustrator Dale Edwin Murray and designer Julia Rosenfeld for sharing their talents with all of us and the world.

Netflix and ITV, our amazing partners with whom we make *Queer Eye*.

Joel Chiodi for overseeing this project on our behalf.

Megan Roth, Rachel Sonis, and the entire Penguin team for their vision.

Margaret Riley King, Nir Caspi, and everyone who works on our behalf at WME.

The full team at Scout Productions for all the love and care they give all our projects.